Baritone B.C.

Light Concert Collection

22 Full Band Arrangements Correlated to *Accent on Achievement*

John O'Reilly and Mark Williams

Contents

Title	Composer	Page
Mary Ann	Williams	2
Sailor's Holiday	Williams	3
Rockin' Candy Mountain	O'Reilly	4
Mucho Mariachi	Williams	5
River Trilogy	O'Reilly	6
Rockin' La Bamba	O'Reilly	7
No Drummer Left Behind	Williams	8
Synco Rock	O'Reilly	9
Canciones Mexicanas	O'Reilly	10
More Cowbell	Williams	11
Skye Boat Song	O'Reilly	12
Two Chinese Folk Songs	O'Reilly	13
Legend of the Alhambra	Williams	14
Pico Rivera	O'Reilly	15
Mountain Songs	Williams	16
African Marching Song	O'Reilly	17
Echoes of Santa Fe	Williams	18
Camino Real	O'Reilly	19
Viva Mariachi	O'Reilly	20
African Spirit Dance	O'Reilly	21
Trumpets of Seville	O'Reilly	22
Stand up and Swing	O'Reilly	23

Alfred Music
P.O. Box 10003
Van Nuys, CA 91410-0003
alfred.com

ISBN-10: 0-7390-9924-8
ISBN-13: 978-0-7390-9924-7

Mary Ann

Jamaican Folk Song
Arranged by Mark Williams
Moderato
mf
Copyright © 2000 by Alfred Music Publishing Co., Inc.
All rights reserved. Printed in USA.

Sailor's Holiday

Mark Williams

Rockin' Candy Mountain

Arranged by John O'Reilly

Mucho Mariachi

Mark Williams

A River Trilogy

Rockin' La Bamba

Arranged by John O'Reilly

No Drummer Left Behind

Mark Williams

Synco-Rock

John O'Reilly

Canciónes Mexicanas
(Mexican Songs)

Arranged by John O'Reilly

More Cowbell

Mark Williams

Skye Boat Song

Scottish Folk Song
Arranged by John O'Reilly

Two Chinese Folk Songs

Legend of the Alhambra

Mark Williams

Pico Rivera

John O'Reilly

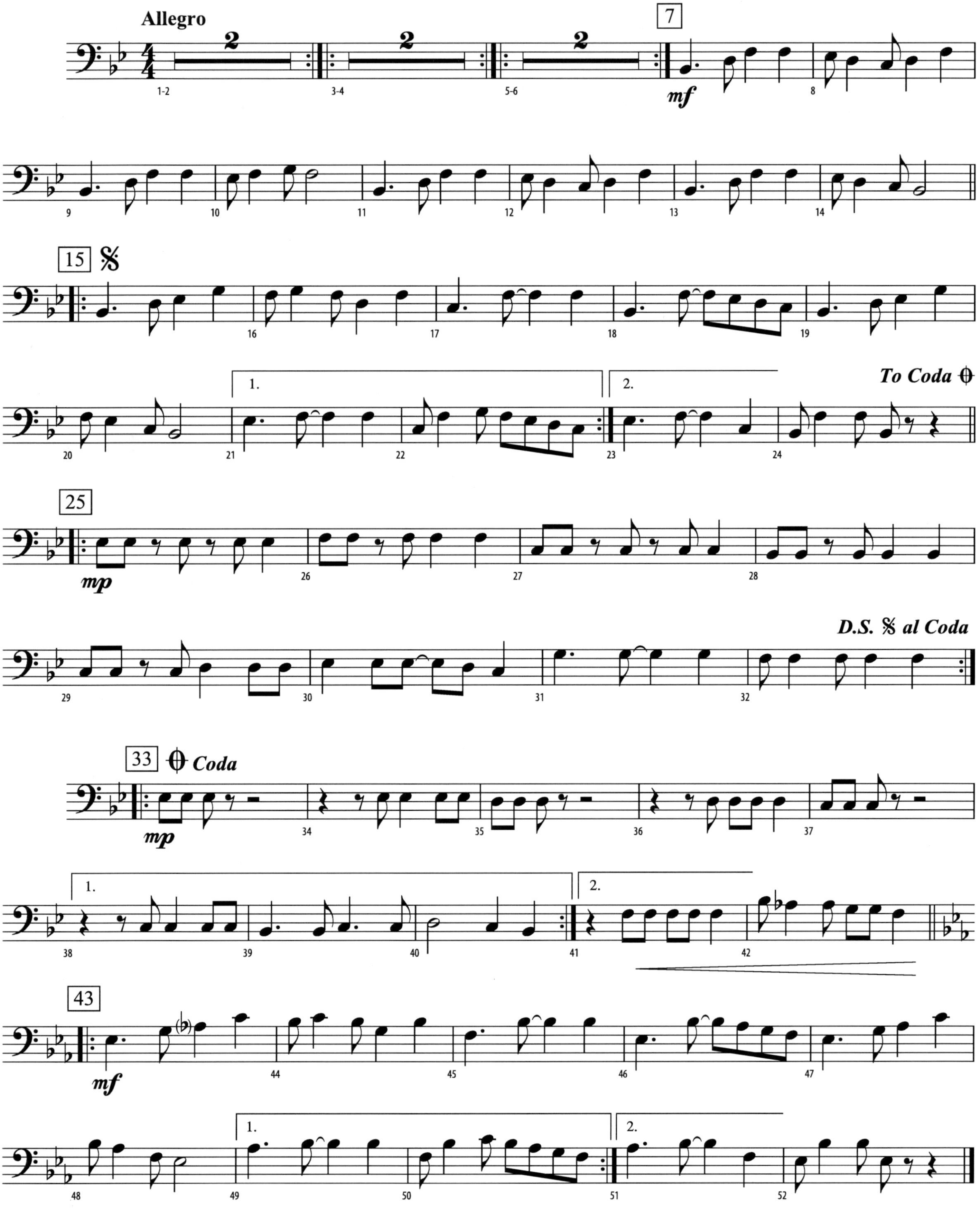
Allegro
7
mf
15
To Coda
25
mp
D.S. al Coda
33
Coda
mp
43
mf
1.
2.

Mountain Songs

Arranged by Mark Williams

African Marching Song
(Siyahamba)

South African Folk Song
Arranged by John O'Reilly

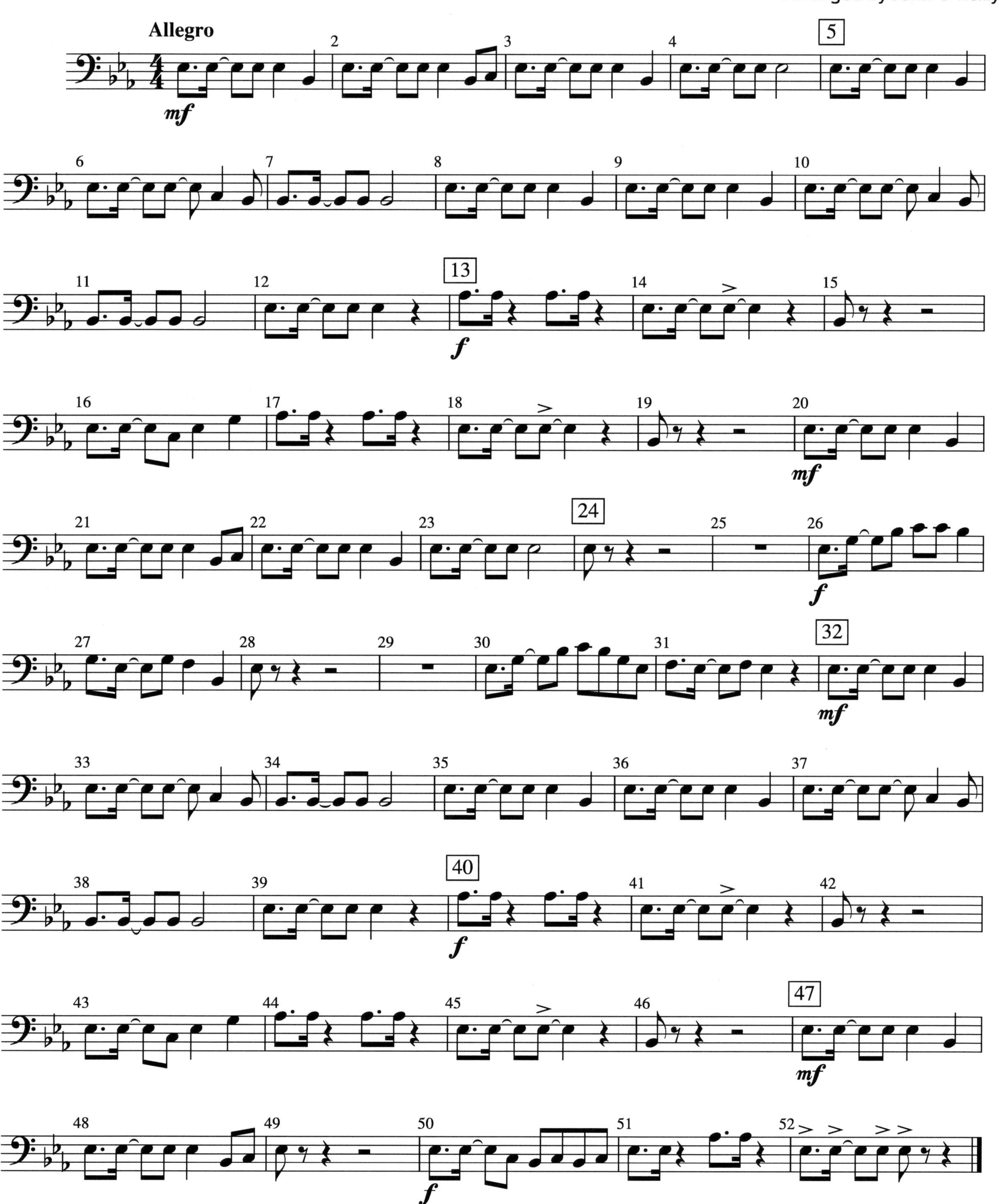

Echoes of Santa Fe

Mark Williams

Camino Real

John O'Reilly

Viva Mariachi

John O'Reilly

African Spirit Dance

John O'Reilly

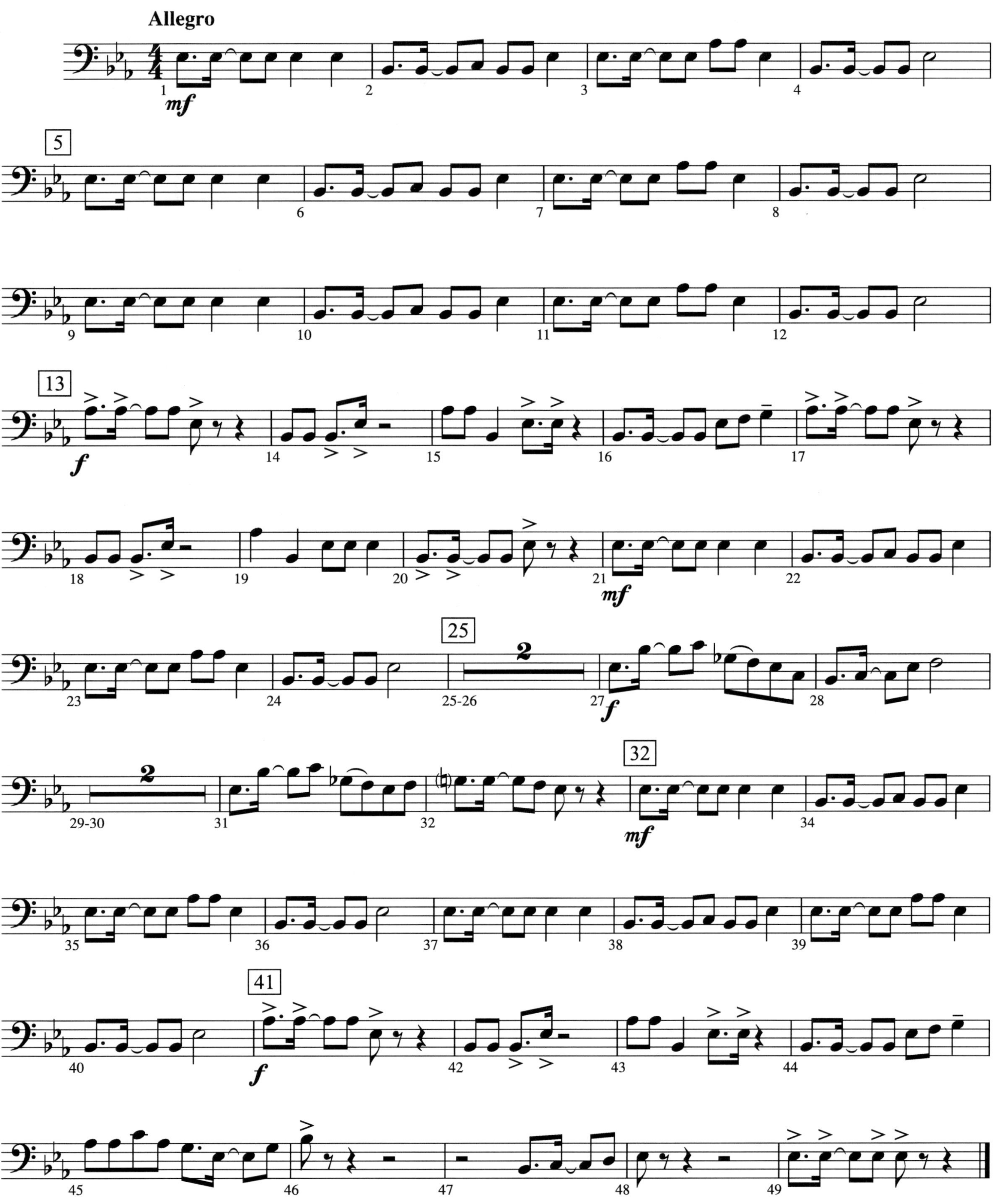

Trumpets of Seville

John O'Reilly

Stand Up and Swing

John O'Reilly